John Burroughs,
THE SAGE OF SLABSIDES

John Burroughs,
THE SAGE OF SLABSIDES

by GINGER WADSWORTH

CLARION BOOKS ❦ New York

Clarion Books
a Houghton Mifflin Company imprint
215 Park Avenue South, New York, NY 10003
Text copyright © 1997 by Ginger Wadsworth
The text for this book is set in 13.5/20-point Centaur.

For information about permission to reproduce selections from this book, write to Permissions,
Houghton Mifflin Company, 215 Park Avenue South, New York, NY 10003.
For information about this and other Houghton Mifflin trade and reference books and multimedia products,
visit The Bookstore at Houghton Mifflin on the World Wide Web at (http://www.hmco.com/trade/).

Printed in the USA

LIBRARY OF CONGRESS CATALOGING-IN-PUBLICATION DATA
Wadsworth, Ginger.
John Burroughs, the sage of Slabsides / by Ginger Wadsworth.
p.   cm.
Includes bibliographical references (p.   ) and index.
Summary: A photobiography of the naturalist, ornithologist, author, poet, teacher, and pioneer
of the conservation movement who lived and worked in his rustic cabin in the Catskill Mountains.
ISBN 0-395-77830-1
1. Burroughs, John, 1837–1921—Juvenile literature.   2. Naturalists—United States—Biography—Juvenile literature.
[1. Burroughs, John, 1837–1921.   2. Naturalists.]   I. Title.
QH31.B93W34   1997
508.73'092—dc20
[B]   95-48400
CIP   AC

HOR   10   9   8   7   6   5   4   3   2   1

To my aunt, Lois Abbott Whitney,
who introduced me to the world of John Burroughs.

—G.W.

One has only to sit down in the woods or the fields, or by the shore of the river or the lake, and nearly everything of interest will come round to him—the birds, the animals, the insects.

"A Sharp Lookout," *Signs and Seasons*

Contents

CHAPTER ONE
Open Country

When John Burroughs was an old man with snowy white hair and a flowing beard, he returned frequently to one of his favorite places in New York's western Catskill Mountains. Just as he had done as a child, he sat on the big red sandstone boulder in the sun and gazed in every direction. All around him, John would write in *My Boyhood*, he saw "open country, like an unrolled map, simple in all its lines."

The Burroughs family farm in the Township of Roxbury, New York. The rock wall fences corralled cows, sheep, and pigs.

The family farm, the Old Home property, stretched below him. Ten miles of stone walls criss-crossed the property. Recalling his farming and fence-building days, he wondered, "How many rocks we turned out of their beds, where they had slept since the great ice sheet tucked them up there, maybe a hundred thousand years ago."

John had remodeled a building on a corner of the Old Home property. Almost every summer from then on, he wrote articles, letters, and new books on the front porch of the house, which he named Woodchuck Lodge, or in his "office," a nearby barn where he had a desk.

John thought about his long career as a nature writer. His ideas about and interest in nature had started on this farm. Now, sixty years later, his books and articles were in homes and schools across America.

The children who had come to see him sat still on the boulder. What were they watching? John wondered. Did they see the clouds dancing across the sky like a flock of newborn lambs? Or the bee gathering pollen in the clover blossom? Or something else?

John reached over to pat one of the farm dogs. Then he stood up. It was time to explore the woods. He hoped the children would hear the song of the hermit thrush, which he called in *Wake-Robin* "the finest sound in nature."

John and one of his dogs in the Riverby vineyards.

CHAPTER TWO

Boyhood

*J*ohn Burroughs was born on April 3, 1837, in northeastern New York state, the seventh of ten children. His parents, Amy and Chauncey Burroughs, owned three hundred acres in the township of Roxbury. Six days a week, from sunrise to sunset, everyone in the family did farm chores.

All the children were expected to do their share of the chores. But John admitted in *My Boyhood*, "I could lean on my fork handle and gaze at the spring landscape. A boy likes almost any work that affords him an escape from routine and humdrum and has an element of play in it."

As a young man, Chauncey Burroughs had red hair and a freckled face. He was seventy-six years old in this picture.

John's mother, Amy Burroughs, at the age of seventy-two. This portrait was taken a few months before her death in 1880.

An avid hunter at that time, he escaped to the woods for long hours, bringing back pigeons, squirrels, partridges, and other wild meat for family meals.

While getting dressed to do his chores, he might notice mud wasps building their nest in the attic. Some mornings, he hurried to his special rock to watch the sunrise. Instead of going straight home, John recalled that he "used to watch and woo the little piping frogs in the spring marshes when I had driven the cows to pasture at night, till they would sit in my open hand and pipe."

This upset his father. When angry, Chauncey Burroughs raised his voice, and everyone on the farm heard him yell. John noted in *Our Friend John Burroughs* that his father's "bark was always to be dreaded," yet confessed that he usually deserved the harsh words.

John's mother often hiked the hills and meadows with her son, letting him escape the drudgery of farm work while they picked wild strawberries and raspberries. Later, John wrote in a letter, "I owe to Mother . . . my love of nature." His Grandfather Kelly, his mother's father, lived only a few miles away and often came to the Home Farm to take his grandson on fishing expeditions to their favorite streams and ponds. John would credit "Granther," as he called him, with teaching him over the years to be an enthusiastic and skilled trout fisherman.

John enjoyed going to school, walking one and a half miles to an old, one-room stone schoolhouse. First, he learned the alphabet, separating consonants from vowels. Before long, he could read. Big words, like *Encyclopaedia Britannica,* fascinated him. Even though he didn't always know what they meant, he repeated them over and over again.

John's first school, called the "Old Stone Jug" by the children.

The family owned few books, so John borrowed books from the district library. He read about history and geography. His favorite book was a story of George Washington. At the age of ten, he was attending the West Settlement School, about two miles from home. A brook flowed past the school, and in the warm months, he and his friends went swimming at recess. On other days, John hurried into the woods to gather wild berries and nuts to add to his "dinner basket" from home.

"Natural history," he reminisced in *My Boyhood*, "was a subject unknown to me . . . and such a thing as nature study in the schools was of course unheard of. Our natural history we got unconsciously at noon time, or on our way to and from school or in our Sunday excursions."

On Sundays, when the family rested and attended a long church service, John played in the woods and fields. He liked to climb the flanks of Old Clump, a mountain behind the farm. In the summers, he followed the streams and spent time building a swimming hole. Except for a dog or two at his side, John enjoyed being alone. There was so much to see and do.

John was different from his brothers and sisters. They didn't share in his interest in the out-of-doors. As John recalled in *Our Friend John Burroughs*, "I had more interests outside my special duties as a farm boy. I loved to roam the hills and woods and prowl along the streams, just to come in contact with the wild and the adventurous."

Although John's father had taught school, Chauncey Burroughs limited his reading to the Bible, a weekly paper, and a religious newspaper. Amy Burroughs could read, but had to spend all her time cooking, making candles and soap, knitting, mending, and doing other endless farm chores. During the winter months, John's brothers and sisters attended school, but like most farm children, they dropped out to help at home. Abigail, one of John's sisters, showed the most interest in reading. However, as his father often said, John was the only one of his children who "took to larnin'."

CHAPTER THREE

World in a Train Whistle

When John was about twelve, he went on his first trip. He and his father traveled fifty miles to the town of Catskill, on the Hudson River. Their wagon was filled with about two thousand pounds of butter. At the dock, John's father sold the forty tubs of butter for about three hundred dollars.

While watching the Hudson River flow toward the sea, John saw his first steamboat. Later, he heard a train whistle. As the empty wagon rolled back home, John knew that someday he wanted to ride on a train and see the rest of the world.

This dream persisted. John sensed the widening gap between himself and his family. Chauncey Burroughs could not see the natural beauty of the world along their route. Instead, he worried about the price of butter and keeping up with the never-ending farm work.

Over the next few years, John grew strong. After a full day of farm work, he read borrowed books by candlelight. But there were endless chores. John churned milk into butter, helped with the haying, and chopped wood to burn in the kitchen stove. He learned to shear the wool off the sheep.

John enjoyed helping his father and brothers tap maple trees for their sugar. He would listen for the first spring calls of the bluebirds, nuthatches, and song sparrows. In late March or early April, he cooked the sap into maple sugar cakes. Later, he carried them in a basket through the fields and woods to the village of Roxbury, a mile or two away. He sold his cakes for two cents each. With his own money, John began to buy used books. One was about geology, the study of rocks; another was a songbook of African-American music.

At the age of sixteen, John graduated from the West Settlement school. Although he loved the farm and his family, John could not imagine growing up to become a farmer. He longed to know more. He was "in many respects an odd one in [his] family . . . like a graft from some other tree." He dreamed of continuing his education, but there wasn't any money for extra schooling.

Carrying a small black bag in his hand, with a few dollars in his pocket and a lump in his throat, John left the Old Home farm in 1854 to teach. His first job was in the village of Tongore, about thirty miles from home, with a starting pay of about eleven dollars a month.

John became a teacher at seventeen. This is one of his schools, in Tongore, New York, about thirty miles from Roxbury.

By the fall of 1854, he had saved enough money from teaching to enroll for one term at the Hedding Literary Institute in Ashland, New York. John studied math, chemistry, Latin, French, and English literature. During this time, his teachers praised his writing, but told him to improve his spelling. Certain words, like *separate, vegetable,* and *mosquito,* were his downfall. John recorded in his pocket-size writing tablet that "I was reading and thinking and trying to get hold of myself. I suppose I was growing all the time."

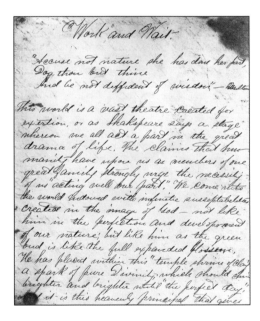 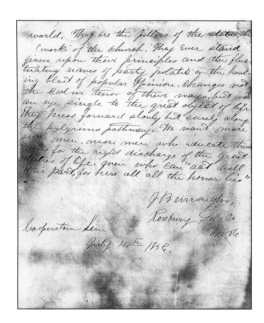

"Work and Wait," an early essay John wrote at the Cooperstown Seminary.

Out of money by April 1855, he returned to teaching and farm work. A year later, he attended Cooperstown Seminary, another college preparatory school. John continued to write and was the best student in composition. He published his first newspaper article on May 13, 1856, under the pen name *Philomath*, which means a lover of learning. Besides schoolwork, John enjoyed exploring the woods. He rowed on a nearby lake and played a new game, called baseball. The term at Cooperstown ended late in the summer, and so did John's formal education.

Once again, he turned to farm work and teaching. Every time he taught at a new school, John had to "board 'round," which meant staying with a different family each month. He met many new people, including Ursula North, the daughter of a farmer in the village of Tongore.

From the start, John admired Ursula. She had dark, curly hair, rosy cheeks, and a trim figure. She seemed sure of herself and wasn't shy. In his notebook, he wrote over and over again *Miss Ursula North.* When John went to another town to teach, he corresponded with Ursula.

Ursula was attracted to the handsome teacher with blue-gray eyes, straight brown eyebrows, and wavy brown hair. John knew so much about the world through his books. Like John, Ursula did not want to live on a farm. She sent him letters written in blue ink on thin white sheets of paper.

CHAPTER FOUR

Ursula

*J*ohn and Ursula had fallen in love. They decided to get married. Ursula wanted John to be a businessman. She pictured them living in a fine house in a busy town. John wanted to become a writer and stated in his notebook, "I . . . have been trying to string . . . sentences together. . . . I suppose that is the way many begin to write." Despite the big difference between their hopes for the future, they were married on September 12, 1857.

This daguerreotype of John, taken when he was twenty, was his first picture. Ursula didn't like his long locks, so John cut his hair

John taught when he could, and during the summer, helped out on his parents' farm. After work, he read books on philosophy and history, plays by Shakespeare, poetry and literature by American authors, such as Edgar Allan Poe, Henry David Thoreau, and Ralph Waldo Emerson. He dipped his pen in a bottle of ink and filled sheets of paper with his thoughts. Ursula complained bitterly. She didn't like her husband's "scribbling."

John continued to write, but to escape Ursula, he "used to go up in the attic and sit on the stairs, using the top step for [a] desk, and getting light from a little window." Strongly influenced by Emerson, a New England philosopher and poet, John wrote about nature. Some of his pieces were printed in small literary magazines, but he was seldom paid. In 1860, he sold "Expressions" to the *Atlantic Monthly*, a well-known literary magazine. Reviewers compared his style to Emerson's. A few years later, John met Emerson and recorded in his journal that the philosopher's "words were like sunshine to my pale and tender genius."

During this time, John made new friends who were interested in nature. While with them on hikes and camping trips, he studied the birds and plants. For the first time, he began to think of himself as a naturalist. In a library at West Point Military Academy, while he was teaching nearby, he discovered artist John James Audubon's *The Birds of America*. Audubon's large, colorful drawings showed the birds in their natural environment. Suddenly, John realized that he wanted his own writing, whether about trees, bees, or birds, to have the same focus.

Tired of teaching for low pay, John moved to Washington, D.C., in 1863 when he was twenty-six. He had heard from friends that he would find a good job there and meet interesting people. Although the Civil War had started in 1860, John had little desire to become a soldier.

In Washington, John found work at the Treasury Department, earning about $1,200 a year. He sent for Ursula, and they rented a two-story brick house in town, near Capitol Hill. They grew most of their own produce on the surrounding acre and kept chickens and a milk cow, called Chloe. Hoping to save some money to buy a house, they took in two boarders.

Every morning, John walked a mile to his office, where he guarded an iron safe filled with about fifty million dollars' worth of banknotes. No one could enter or leave without his permission.

John wasn't that busy at work. Most days, he sat for long hours on a high stool in front of a large mahogany desk. To pass the time, he penned short pieces, called essays, about one idea or subject. He rewrote them and rewrote them. As he did, John began to create his own style of writing.

He sold some of these essays to the *Atlantic Monthly*. In "With the Birds," later published in *Wake-Robin*, John told about the gnatcatcher that "mews like a young kitten, erects its tail, flirts, droops its wings, goes through a variety of motions when disturbed by your presence."

In another essay, "In the Hemlocks," John said:

> I walk along the old road, and note the tracks in the thin layer
> of mud. . . . Here a partridge has set its foot; there, a woodcock;
> here, a squirrel or mink; there, a skunk; there a fox . . . how easy
> to distinguish it from that of a little dog. . . . There is as much
> wildness in the track of an animal as in its voice.

Readers enjoyed John's articles and were glad when the *Atlantic Monthly* decided to publish several more.

As he walked to work and back, John often passed platoons of soldiers with swords and rifles. Cannons boomed in the distance. Horse-drawn ambulances carried wounded soldiers into the city. Sometimes, President Abraham Lincoln passed by, wearing his black silk hat.

Despite the war, John was happy. He loved to wander into the woods surrounding Washington, D.C. To Myron Benton, a poet friend, he wrote:

> I saw and heard the fox sparrow sing—a round, firm note, reminding one of the oriole—and the gray Titmouse whistle. The purple finch sang also, the robin piped, the bluebird carolled, the snow-bird lisped, the great wren warbled, and the song sparrow sang. You see I am quite mad, and still on the subject of birds.

John enjoyed meeting people who were interested in books, writing, and nature. One of his new friends, Walt Whitman, was a published poet. His *Leaves of Grass* had been reprinted for the third time. Whitman encouraged John to keep on writing, especially about country life. He told John to find his own voice.

An engraving of Walt Whitman. He and John became friends when they both lived in Washington, D.C. Walt appreciated Ursula's cooking and showed up on Sundays for her pancake breakfasts.

The Civil War fighting, which John wrote about in letters home, moved closer to Washington, D.C. One evening, John put on the blue uniform of a Treasury guard and walked with a friend to a battle-field to see the war up close. In the darkness, he lay in a trench. Bullets whizzed past him. He saw blood and dead soldiers. It was an experience he would never forget.

A few weeks later, on April 9, 1865, the city's bells began to ring. The Civil War had ended, and so had slavery. President Lincoln was assassinated a few days later.

Walt Whitman wrote "When Lilacs Last in the Dooryard Bloom'd," a mournful poem about Lincoln's death. Taking John's advice, he had a hermit thrush sing a solemn and sweet song through-out the poem.

Following the war, the Burroughses remained in Washington, D.C. In 1867, the American News Company in New York published John's first book, *Notes on Walt Whitman as Poet and Person.* He paid most of the publishing costs himself. Piles of unsold copies filled the parlor, and Ursula grumbled about dusting the many books.

CHAPTER FIVE

A Way of Thinking

At his desk in the Treasury Building, John returned to nature writing, planning one book on birds and another of farm sketches. In 1871, Hurd & Houghton (later Houghton Mifflin Company) published *Wake-Robin*, a collection of John's essays which are mainly about birds. The Introduction summed up John's way of thinking:

> If I name every bird I see in my walk, describe its color and ways, etc., give a lot of facts or details about the bird, it is doubtful if my reader is interested. But if I relate the bird in some way to human life, to my own life—show what it is to me and what it is in the landscape and the season—then do I give my reader a live bird and not a labeled specimen.

He didn't use scientific words to explain nature, but just wrote about what he saw, usually adding a bit of humor. Everyday readers felt as though they were going on a little trip with John and identified with him when he wrote in one story that "My hands and wrists suddenly began to smart and itch. . . . Then the smarting extended to my neck and face, even to my scalp." Later on, they learned how John escaped the thirsty mosquitoes by wrapping himself in a buffalo robe and dozing all night long on a flat rock.

Wake-Robin was an instant success. All across America, readers agreed with William Dean Howells, editor of the *Atlantic Monthly*, that reading *Wake-Robin* "is a sort of summer vacation." John and his publisher decided to do another book.

Tired of city life, John quit his job at the Treasury Department. He had always dreamed of a home in the country. First, he found a part-time job as a bank examiner for several districts north of New York City and in Virginia. Early in 1873, he bought nine acres of farmland on the west shore of the Hudson River in New York. There were fields already planted with fruit trees, grapes, and berry vines. The woods, of ash, maple, and butternut trees, and a nearby stream would attract birds.

Excited about the changes, John wrote Walt Whitman that "I can make more money here, be much freer." Roxbury was about fifty miles away, so he could visit his parents at the Old Home farm several times a year.

Walt Whitman with a butterfly on his finger. He stayed with the Burroughses at Riverby. John called the nearby woods "Whitman Land" in honor of walks they took there.

John wore a suit and vest to work with a gold watch tucked in his pocket, but preferred more casual clothing.

Ursula, or Sulie as John called her, enjoyed city life in Washington, D.C.

John wrote Ursula, who waited in Washington, D.C., "I have made a plan of our house. It is half wood and half stone." Over the following months, John and his workmen finished the three-story building, later named Riverby. Ursula looked forward to running her new home. As John had promised her, it would have many rooms, a balcony, and a hall with a curving staircase to make an impressive entrance to the house. Ursula planned a vegetable garden and a rose bed like ones she'd left in Washington, D.C.

John and Ursula moved in at the end of 1874. It didn't take them long to discover that the big house was gloomy and drafty. The small oval windows John had selected for some rooms didn't let in much light. The library wasn't inviting because the fireplace didn't work well. John was also disappointed in his study. Although it had a balcony and a view of the hills to the west, the room was cold and dark in the winter.

Riverby, north of Poughkeepsie on the western shore of the Hudson River, was John and Ursula's home for nearly sixty years.

Despite these problems, John published his second book of essays, *Winter Sunshine*, in 1875. In one essay called "The Apple," John wrote that "The apple is the commonest and yet the most varied and beautiful of fruits. How pleasing to touch! I toy with you; press your face to mine, toss you in the air, roll you on the ground, see you shine. You are so alive! You glow like a ruddy flower."

When he wasn't writing or working at his part-time job, he tilled the soil and planted grapevine seedlings. The sun tanned his skin; streaks of white began to mark his brown beard. Over the years, he planted thousands of currants and raspberries, too. But grapes were John's largest crop and required constant watching to make sure the birds didn't eat the fruit. Each year, if his vineyard survived blizzards, disease, and hungry birds, John and his helpers harvested tons of grapes. In 1891, he would ship out twenty-one tons of fruit.

Ursula was equally busy. Riverby, with the kitchen on the lowest floor and the bedrooms on the third floor, was hard to clean. Ursula spent long hours going up and down the stairs with her scrubbing brushes and mops. Dusting, sweeping, and laundry filled her life. As usual, the Burroughses clashed on how clean the house should be, and John wrote Myron Benton that "Even the cat wipes her feet on the mat before she ventures inside."

Despite their active lives, John and Ursula were lonely. They dreamed of having children to fill the large house. In the meantime, they formed strong bonds with a series of farm dogs, starting with one called Rab. After Rab died, John buried him next to a rock near a spring on the property and recorded, "I may live to be an old man, but I shall not live long enough to forget Rab. He has been the life and light of the place for a year."

His next dog, Rosemary Rose, often went with him in his buggy to various bank jobs, or on tramps in the woods. John walked all over the countryside to try to study every bird, insect, and flower. His goal was to learn and understand the natural world. When Rosemary Rose died, a new dog, named Lark, joined John in his strolls. Now, as he recorded in his journal, "I walk four miles in great glee, my dog and I." Another entry said, "All the landscape for miles and miles we have read over and over, as two boys read a story-book."

A farm dog, 'I-know,' was "very intelligent and handsome, and gentle as a lamb. Even the cats imposed upon him and made a rug of him," John recorded in his journal.

Although John always jotted down his thoughts, debts, and even grocery lists, he decided to become more organized. He purchased several inexpensive notebooks filled with lined paper. For the rest of his life, he would record his nature-related thoughts in these notebooks.

On July 1, 1878, John sat down in his study and wrote in his journal: "Baby came to-day—a great event." After twenty years of marriage, John and Ursula adopted a child. They named him Julian.

Shortly after Julian arrived, his proud parents took him to Roxbury to meet his grandparents and the rest of the Burroughs family. A few weeks later, Ursula's father came to Riverby to see his new grandson.

John noted in his journal, "Julian . . . and I walk up to the post office. See the honey bees working on the pussy willows. Walk back on the railroad track. Paint and fix our boat."

Eight years later, Ursula would learn that John was Julian's natural father. His birth mother had been a housemaid at Riverby named Amanda Henion. After Ursula demanded the truth, John wrote in his journal about "a domestic storm for several days and nights; all about Julian," and another entry stating "earthquake shocks still pretty severe." From the very beginning, Ursula loved Julian, so in time, she accepted the situation. A devoted father, John wrote a friend that Julian "and I have great times already."

John continued to keep up his journal. Some of his "Spring Jottings" were later published in his book *Riverby*:

MARCH 3. The sun is getting strong, but winter still holds his own. The first bluebird note this morning. How sweetly it dropped down from the blue overhead!

MARCH 10. A real spring day at last . . . bees very lively about the hive.

MARCH 12. A delicious spring morning. Hundreds of snowbirds with a sprinkling of song and Canada sparrows are all about the house, chirping and lisping and chattering. . . .

MARCH 24. Damp, still morning, much fog on the river. All the branches and twigs of the trees strung with drops of water. The grass and weeds beaded with fog drops. Two lines of ducks go up the river, one a few feet beneath the other.

APRIL 1. The month of the swelling buds, the springing grass, the first nests, the first plants, the first flowers.

APRIL 2. How I like to walk out after supper these days! An April twilight is unlike any other.

APRIL 8. A day of great brightness and clearness. . . . The smoke from the chimney goes straight up.

APRIL 13. These days the song of the toad—tr-r-r-r-r-r-r-r-r-r-r-r— is heard in the land. At nearly all hours I hear it, and it is as welcome to me as the song of any bird.

APRIL 21. The enchanting days continue without a break. One's senses are not large enough to take them all in.

CHAPTER SIX

Fame . . . So This Is Fame

*J*ohn's journal entries grew into essays. Many were about birds. In "Winter Neighbors," John chopped down a rotten apple tree, only to discover a little red owl, probably an Eastern Screech Owl, lying in the chips of wood as though dead. John pulled the owl free by a wing, but the bird "suddenly transformed into another creature. His eyes flew wide open, his talons clutched my fingers . . . and every motion and look said, 'Hands off, at your peril.'" The owl soon began to "play possum" again. John kept the sleeping owl in a covered woodbox, dropping in a live mouse from time to time. "There would be a sudden rustle in the box, a faint squeak, and then silence. After a week of captivity I gave [the owl] his freedom in the full sunshine. . . . Just at dusk in the winter nights, I often hear his soft bur-r-r-r, very pleasing and bell-like." John undoubtedly hoped that the owl had moved into a new winter home in a tree hole.

By 1879, John had two new books: *Birds and Poets* and *Locusts and Wild Honey*. One of his most popular essays, "Strawberries," appeared in *Locusts and Wild Honey*. John wrote, "Indeed the strawberry belongs to the juiciest time of the year. What a challenge it is to the taste! Is there anything like the odor of strawberries? The next best thing to tasting them is to smell them."

John and Julian fished and boated on the Pepacton River. Old Clump (now Burroughs Mountain) rises in the background.

Besides writing and working in the vineyard, John explored the surrounding woods and fields. He visited his parents on the Old Home farm. Sometimes, he escaped with Julian to go camping in the Catskills, often in a valley near Slide Mountain. He might climb to the top of Slide or Wittenberg Mountain, two of his favorite places.

Visitors came to Riverby. Some were authors; others just wanted to meet John. Fans sought his advice on nature or shared their own experiences in the out-of-doors. They knew of his writing through magazines like the *Atlantic Monthly, The North American Review, Century Magazine,* and *Country Life,* as well as through his steady stream of books following *Wake-Robin.*

Ursula still did not approve of her husband's writing. John's books sold well, but they only gave him a small royalty, which he took as a yearly stipend. At first, it was $500 (although by 1912, he received $2,000 a year from Houghton Mifflin). According to one story, after a group of visitors had gone home, Ursula angrily swept a floor, mumbling, "Fame . . . fame . . . so this is fame."

Ringing a bell, she summoned John to do household chores for her. One day, John decided he needed a more peaceful workplace. In 1881, he had a small house constructed down the hill toward the river. He covered the exterior with thick chestnut bark and called it his "Bark Study." From the windows, John watched the boats on the Hudson River and his vineyard stretching to the shore. Woodpeckers tapped on the roof and the sides of his study in search of worms and bugs. A constant reader, John lined his bookshelves with a wide range of subjects from Greek philosophy to Charles Darwin's theory of evolution to poetry collections.

John wrote that some birds thought that his Bark Study was "a huge stump that ought to hold fat grubs." They pecked so loudly that he came to the door, expecting to see human visitors.

Often ignoring Ursula's demands to help with chores, John penned dozens of essays in his study. One was about a little gray rabbit: "I think I can feel her good-will through the floor, and I hope she can mine. When I have a happy thought, I imagine her ears twitch, especially when I think of the sweet apple I will place by her doorway at night."

"Winter Neighbors" and twelve other essays were published in *Signs and Seasons*. Once again, readers enjoyed John's new book because it was about the simple life during a changing time in America. Since the end of the Civil War, the country was experiencing the Industrial Revolution. New machines, such as printing presses and engines, were being invented. More people, including immigrants from other countries, were crowding into cities. And railroads crisscrossed the land, making it easier for people to travel from city to city without exploring the remaining open spaces. John's books reminded readers that they should and could still connect with the natural world.

Although he had written eight popular books, John still didn't enjoy Ursula's respect. He noted in his journal that "Mrs. B. advises me to give up writing and do something else for a living."

It was a busy time at Riverby. Julian was an active eight-year-old. While Ursula kept the house clean and orderly, John tended to his fruit trees, grapevines, and vegetables. He also raised chickens and kept bees on the Riverby property, which had expanded to twenty acres. When his bank job ended, John devoted more time to his writing.

In January of 1887, Ursula rented rooms in nearby Poughkeepsie so that Julian could attend school there. She liked making friends and being part of the community's social activities. From time to time, John joined Ursula and Julian in Poughkeepsie, but he preferred to write and read in the quiet that Riverby now provided him.

Teachers were starting to read John's books to their students. Children also read his stories in their favorite magazines: *Youth's Companion* and *St. Nicholas.* Many of his essays were about birds. In "The Spring Bird Procession," later collected in *Field and Study,* he described the nuthatches:

> Soft-voiced, soft-colored, gentle-mannered, they glide over the rough branches and the tree-trunks with their boat-shaped bodies, going up and down and around, with apparently an extra joint in their necks that enables them, head-downward, to look straight out from the tree-trunk.

John's fame continued to grow. He probably had more mail than any previous American author had ever received. He walked to the post office to collect it. Fans sent him birds, flowers, or insects from around the world to identify. Others asked for his autograph, a photograph, a handwritten poem, and his views on a variety of subjects.

In 1888, teacher Mary E. Burt started a movement that was to spread across the country. She asked the Chicago School Board to buy extra copies of *Pepacton,* John's adventures on his homemade

John talked to some school children at the Tongore schoolhouse where he taught as a young man.

boat down the Pepacton River, a tributary of the Delaware River. The first few pages of the book captured students' attention:

> When my boat was finished—and it was a very simple affair—I was as eager as a boy to be off; I feared the river would all run by before I could wet her bottom in it. I stuck on a rift before I had gone ten yards, and saw . . . the paint transferred from my little scow [boat] to the tops of the stones. . . . But I was soon making fair headway, and taking trout for my dinner as I floated along.

"Baba" was popular with his granddaughters, Betty and Ursula. He enjoyed reading to them, just as he had enjoyed reading Grimm's Fairy Tales and other books to Julian.

After finishing *Pepacton*, students sought other Burroughs books, claiming his stories were more interesting than those in their readers. Hearing this, Oscar Houghton, John's editor at Houghton Mifflin Company, decided to publish a small book of John's stories, called *Birds and Poets*.

Before long, children from coast to coast were enjoying *Birds and Poets*, *Pepacton*, and everything else they could find by John Burroughs. Houghton Mifflin Company published other Burroughs readers for children. For the first time, many teachers started nature-study lessons in their classrooms. Children collected bird feathers and interesting rocks to share in school. They purchased magnifying glasses and learned to "look at the body of a fly . . . or at the speck of an insect" as John did in *The Summit of the Years*.

Nature clubs, including one called the John Burroughs Society, sprang up across the country, encouraging the study of nature in homes and extending it to more schools. John visited several schools and listened to the students read from his books.

On the weekends, families left the cities to try hiking and camping. They looked forward to sleeping under the stars. Inspired by John's experiences, they hoped to discover a hummingbird's nest, eat berries in the woods, and turn over stones. In *Leaf and Tendril*, they had read about how "the crickets and ants and beetles would rush about" as well as how they might uncover the home of "a blinking, bead-eyed, meadow-mouse."

CHAPTER SEVEN

An Army of Nature Students🖙

*W*henever John met a young person carrying camping gear, he was thrilled. As one friend noted in a letter, later published in *Speaking for Nature* by Paul Brooks, John had created "an army of nature-students" with his books. Many of these students, and those of future generations, would be activists in the conservation movement.

John and his friend, writer Hamlin Garland, share in the planting of a tree.

Even teachers sought his advice. One asked how to plant a tree for Arbor Day. John's letter replied, "Give the tree . . . a soft, deep bed to rest in; tuck it up very carefully in its bed with your hands. The roots of a tree are much more soft and tender than its branches . . . when you plant a tree with love, it always lives."

Young women began to study nature in college and join outdoor-oriented clubs. Vassar College students organized the Wake-Robin Bird Club, named in honor of John's first book of essays. Many were training to be teachers, and enjoyed bird-watching. With their teachers, they came by train or took a little freight steamer up and across the Hudson River to Riverby. At the sight of John Burroughs on the dock, they waved their handkerchiefs, then stepped ashore. John led them up the hill, stopping to point out the birds and identify their songs, teach the students how to make penholders from dried stalks of cattails, and show them plants, like pink lady's slippers and showy white orchids.

At Slabsides, a group of Vassar students from the Wake-Robin Club listen carefully to John's stories.

John would be associated with Vassar for over forty years. During the winter months, he joined Ursula in their rented rooms in the city of Poughkeepsie, where Vassar was located, because Riverby was so hard to heat. John made many friends on the staff and attended functions on the campus.

Over the years, John's books brought him admirers of all ages. One friend, Theodore Roosevelt,

John and President Theodore Roosevelt at their campsite in Yellowstone Park, 1903. John liked Roosevelt, he told a friend in a letter, because "he always has time to talk of birds and animals."

John Burroughs and John Muir joined Edward H. Harriman's scientific expedition to Alaska in 1899. Here, they are standing on Muir Glacier.

would become the president of the United States. Another friend was John Muir. A naturalist, Muir lived in California and was an expert on the West. The two "Johns" visited each other in their home states. They traveled together to Alaska and the Grand Canyon and talked about writing.

Other authors, including Olive Thorne Miller (*Bird-Ways*) and Neltje Blanchan Doubleday (*Bird Neighbors*) were influenced by John Burroughs. They wrote about nature, especially about birds. The Audubon Society, of which John was a vice president in 1897, reached out to teachers and students through its popular magazine, *Bird Lore*.

Every year, John's popularity increased. He received honorary degrees from two colleges. He lectured, too, to women's clubs, a teachers' training school, and high school groups. But being famous embarrassed him. In a letter to a friend, later published in *Speaking for Nature*, he wrote that "I always feel a little sheepish when I am much praised."

Although John Burroughs enjoyed travel, he loved to be at Riverby and the nearby Catskill Mountains. But home wasn't always peaceful. At times, parades of uninvited visitors showed up at Riverby. They wanted to meet John Burroughs and see his Bark Study. Once again, John decided he needed to escape—this time, he admitted, from the grandeur of his river view and the grape vineyard.

John purchased twenty acres of land in the woods, about a mile and a half west of Riverby. He liked being in his beloved woods where he tramped and studied nature so often. Before long, he dreamed of building a cabin that would be a guest house for his friends and also a writing retreat. On November 25, 1895, he and some helpers began to build a two-story cabin nestled close to a sheltering cliff wall in the woods. The outer walls were slabs—cut logs with the bark left on. A sloping roof protected the porch from the weather; a great stone chimney heated the interior. John gathered limbs and tree trunks to make rustic beds, cabinets, and tables. He named his new house Slabsides.

Hauling water from a spring at Slabsides.

John and his brother Hiram at Slabsides. Once John told a group of visitors, "I am a good cook but a poor housekeeper! I scrubbed the floor of Slabsides—once. It took me two hours, but before the floor was dry my brother Hiram walked over it with muddy shoes. . . . I never again laid myself open to a similar temptation."

On April 18, 1896, he set up housekeeping in the cabin. Hiram, his oldest brother, soon joined him. A quiet man, Hiram worked with John at farming, kept bees and chickens, and stayed there until his health failed. He died in 1902.

After draining a swampy area, John planted thirty thousand celery plants in long rows in the rich black soil. One year, he sold the celery to make some much-needed extra cash, since his grape crop at Riverby had been destroyed by a hail-and-rain storm.

Sometimes, John spent only a few hours a day at Slabsides. Other times, when he didn't stay at Riverby with Ursula or travel, he might live in the small cabin for several weeks.

John and Francis Fisher Browne, the editor of The Dial, *a literary magazine. Slabsides housed quilts made by Amy Burroughs, a few of her mulberry-pattern dishes, banners from Vassar and Smith Colleges, books, photographs, and birds' nests and other treasures from the woods.*

John always looked forward to returning to Slabsides. As he explained to a friend, "I came up here—to [Slabsides] to get away from paint and polish." Happy and healthy, he wrote when he wanted to, using a pen made from an eagle feather. He filled pads of paper with his ideas, holding the pages down with a flat rock. Other ideas covered envelopes or the edges of newspapers. John even wrote on the walls of Slabsides.

Before long, friends who came to visit were calling John the Sage of Slabsides. Wearing a long apron wrapped around his waist, he cooked homegrown vegetables and broiled steaks in the fireplace on a sharpened stick of maple or black birch. Guests sipped cups of fresh spring water John had hauled inside.

One of his first guests was John Muir. The two men sat up late by the fire, swapping stories about their favorite dogs and their adventures in Alaska. During his college vacations, Julian visited Slabsides, too. President and Mrs. Theodore Roosevelt also came for dinner one hot summer day in 1903. The two men sat on the porch, joined by Mrs. Roosevelt, talking about many subjects, including their common interest in bird-watching. And later, in dedicating *Outdoor Pastimes of an American Hunter* to John, President Roosevelt said: "It is a good thing for our people that you have lived."

Visitors, invited and uninvited, continued to climb the hill to Slabsides. Over the next twenty years, about seven thousand people signed John's guest book. Sometimes, John chatted with members of the Wake-Robin Bird Club from Vassar College, who came frequently to Slabsides.

John and a group of Vassar students on a picnic following a walk in the woods where he helped them identify bird songs and find nests.

Following a walk in the woods, they might picnic with John by Black Creek Falls. On another day, a group of Boy Scouts might climb the steps to the porch to ask John's help in identifying a bird's nest. Always a natural teacher, John didn't mind putting down his pen to spend time with young people. Other times, he picked up his pen to answer his mail. A typical fan letter opened with:

I am a boy seventeen years old and I live out here on the prairies of the Dakotas on a claim. I am a farmer's boy. I would like very much to become a naturalist, and write about birds and nature like you.

When I read your book [*Fresh Fields*, 1884] it seems just like I've found a friend at last who don't think a person's odd because he loves to ramble in the woods.

John's answer read in part, "My Dear Young Friend, Keep your eyes and ears open, read the best books, and practice writing whenever you have something you want to say." Orland E. White listened to John's advice and went on to college, later becoming the curator of plants at the Brooklyn Botanic Garden in New York.

CHAPTER EIGHT

A New Century, a New Friend

*B*esides answering letters and writing about birds, John wrote of many things: literature, philosophy, and his travels to England, Jamaica, and other parts of the United States, especially the West. In *The Light of Day*, he attacked organized religion. John also wrote critical essays about writers he labeled as "nature fakers" because they mixed fact and fiction, giving animals human emotions such as sorrow, revenge, and rage. His favorite subject, though, was birds in their natural settings. As he told his friend Myron Benton in a letter, "My wife is always pointing out the bird's nest in my hair, but she doesn't see deep enough—it is in my brain."

This 1918 illustration by F. Foster Lincoln in Life *magazine portrayed John as a friend to all wildlife.*

John journeyed west and visited the Grand Canyon with John Muir. Taking the four-foot-wide Bright Angel Trail, they rode mules into the mile-deep canyon and back up again.

With the start of the twentieth century, John saw and commented about the world's fast-changing ways. Before long, Americans would travel from city to city by cars, on highways. And in 1903, the Wright brothers successfully flew in an airplane.

John also witnessed a series of legislative acts, starting in 1872, in which wilderness areas like Yosemite and the Grand Canyon were preserved as national parks. Some of the credit, he knew, belonged to his good friends John Muir and President Roosevelt.

In May 1901, a month after his sixty-fourth birthday, John opened a letter that would influence the rest his life. It was from Dr. Clara Barrus, a thirty-seven-year-old psychiatrist in Middletown, New York. For years, she had admired his books and his views on life. They started to correspond. Then Dr. Barrus visited Slabsides.

The visit firmly established their friendship. Clara moved closer to John and they saw each other every day. Ursula liked Clara. In his journal, John described his friend: "A very keen, appreciative mind . . . the most companionable woman I have yet met in this world—reads and delights in the same books I do—a sort of feminine counterpart of myself."

Clara began to help John with typing, editing, and proofreading his manuscripts, starting with *Literary Values,* a criticism of the academic world, and then typed a biography of John James Audubon. With Clara's help, John would continue to write a new book every year or two. They had known each other only five months when Clara became his official biographer. John sent her all his journals through the 1880s with a note, dated December 7, 1901: "I would like you to have them all when I am gone. I am truly surprised at your interest in them." He also gave her letters, manuscripts, and other treasures of importance.

The following year, in 1902, Julian married Emily Mackay. They lived in The Nest, a house John built for them on the Riverby property. Julian managed the vineyards. They would have three children, Elizabeth, Ursula, and John II. John adored his grandchildren and visited them nearly every day at The Nest, as did Ursula. He filled his journals with tales of Julian and Emily's three children. Drawn together as devoted grandparents, he and Ursula quarreled less often.

Children gather around John and Ursula in front of the Riverby well. John II rides on his grandfather's shoulders.

But John was often away, giving speeches, visiting friends, or traveling. While taking a cross-country trip to Yellowstone National Park with President Roosevelt in 1903, he wrote to Clara on April 5:

> You should have seen the crowds yesterday. . . . At one point . . . I saw a big banner borne by some girls with this inscription, The JOHN BURROUGHS SOCIETY. The girls pushed their way through the crowd and timidly and hurriedly handed me a big bouquet. I could only say "Thank you."

In 1904, John returned to nature writing and published his fifteenth book, *Far and Near*. In an essay called "Wild Life About My Cabin," John described Slabsides: "When I went into the woods the robins went with me, or rather they followed close. As soon as a space of ground was cleared and the garden planted, they were on hand to pick up the worms and insects, and to superintend the planting of the cherry-trees." Two years later, he published *Bird and Bough*, a collection of his poems about flowers and birds.

Although John still liked Slabsides, he began to spend some summers and the fall at a house on the family farm. Clara Barrus often joined him. John called the house Woodchuck Lodge because of the large number of rodents that burrowed in the fields, hillsides, and garden. At night, he set

John with Dr. Clara Barrus, right, and her niece, Harriet Barrus. John's coat, made of woodchuck pelts, is on permanent display at the American Museum of Natural History in New York City.

up a cot on the sleeping porch of the house because he loved to awake to the sunrise. As he told Clara Barrus in *Our Friend John Burroughs,* "And to think I've stayed down there on the Hudson all these years with never the home feeling, when here were my native hills waiting to cradle me as they did in my youth."

Woodchuck Lodge became John's summer home during the last ten years of his life. Woodchucks burrowed in his garden, so he tried to keep their numbers down by shooting them. He remarked that as he "killed one, seven came to the funeral."

John was happy at Woodchuck Lodge. He enjoyed having his daughter-in-law, Emily, bring the children for a visit. Ursula only spent a few weeks at Woodchuck Lodge each summer. Every morning after breakfast, John set off with his market basket full of manuscripts and walked to his office, a weatherworn hay barn facing the woods. His desk was a rough box covered with Manila

Emily, Julian, John, and granddaughters Elizabeth and Ursula (on John's lap) in front of the Bark Study.

paper, and his seat was an old hickory chair. John loved the smell of the hay and the view through the wide doorway. He composed his essays in longhand, telling Julian once in a letter that the typewriter would "get into" the writing if one wasn't careful.

Despite the constant flow of guests at Woodchuck Lodge, John wrote Julian at Riverby in 1911 that he had accomplished more than normal for a summer. He also gave credit to Clara for typing up his essays, some as many as three times, until he was satisfied with their quality. Besides writing, John loved to roam over the pastures, hoe his garden, lie in a hammock under the apple trees, or sit with friends and talk.

CHAPTER NINE

The Simple Life

*N*o matter where he was, John was seldom idle. His philosophy was part of a letter that he wrote to students in New York City. It was read aloud in every public school classroom on his seventy-fourth birthday, April 3, 1911: "With me, the secret of my youth in age is the simple life—simple food, sound sleep, the open air, daily work, kind thoughts, love of nature, and joy and contentment in the world in which I live."

Henry Ford *Thomas Edison* *Harvey Firestone*

A year later, when John turned seventy-five, the American Museum of Natural History in New York gave him a birthday party in the Bird Hall, attended by six hundred children. Children paraded in costumes that represented each one of John's books. John was overcome with tears of joy and noted in his journal that the party was "a great blow-out."

That same year, John met Henry Ford, the car manufacturer. A warm friendship grew between the two men. John, Henry Ford, and his friends Thomas Edison, the inventor, and Harvey Firestone, a manufacturer, went camping together many times. Ford visited John at Slabsides and Woodchuck Lodge, and helped him purchase a few acres surrounding the lodge.

The two friends shared a keen interest in birds. Along the various routes of their camping trips, John gathered flowers and at night wrote letters by campfire about the scenery. In one, he added: "All through Pa. and Maryland and W. VA., in every village where we paused, I met people who had read my books—teachers, pupils, professional men, etc."

John preferred to drive with the top down, letting the wind blow his white whiskers.

Ford even gave John a new car. Used to watching birds and looking at flowers, John forgot at times to keep his eyes on the road and had several accidents. In his journal, he noted: "Have just taken a run of a few miles in the car. The blind, desperate thing still scares me. How ready it is to take to the ditch, or a tree, or the fence." John enjoyed the car, but admitted that he was not a good driver. Before long, Julian and others took over most of the driving.

Sometimes, John traveled with Clara and her nieces. Other times, Ursula joined him. Wherever John went in his later years, fans recognized him. It was hard to miss the elderly man with the white hair and beard. Schoolchildren carried copies of his books for him to autograph. Newspaper reporters interviewed him and took pictures. Crowds met him at train stations. Once, when leaving Pasadena, California, John gathered bouquets of flowers from children. As he stood on the rear platform of the departing train, children sang, waved, cheered, and threw more flowers. At long last, Ursula accepted that her husband was a respected writer around the world.

During 1916, Ursula was not well. The doctors said she had terminal colon cancer. Ursula died a year and a half later on March 6, 1917. John noted in his journal: "A long chapter in my life, nearly sixty years ended. I am too much crushed to write about it now."

The news of World War I—of the collapse of Russia and the success of the Germans—occupied his thoughts and writing most of the time. Every day, he read the war news in the paper. The deaths of thousands of young Americans, including Theodore Roosevelt's son, Quentin, deeply depressed him. John supported President Woodrow Wilson and believed along with Wilson that America's entry into the fighting was the only way to stop Germany. With Germany's defeat, future wars would be prevented and the United States wouldn't have to stockpile weapons. John told his friends and family that world peace would follow, taking a great burden off people everywhere.

Alone at Riverby, he described the stone house as a tomb and wrote, "Oh, the falling leaves!

John at his desk at Slabsides.

Felt her [Ursula's] loss afresh when I went over to the kitchen door and found the leaves clustered there as if waiting for something. They were waiting for her broom."

Approaching the age of eighty-one, and over the immediate grief following Ursula's death, he wrote:

The New Year finds me in pretty good health, writing in the morning, and sawing and splitting wood nearly an hour in [the] afternoon . . . my interest in the War [World War I], in Nature, in books, as keen as ever. Weight about 132. Sight and hearing good, memory a little uncertain. Appetite as good as ever.

The war officially ended on November 11, 1918. Church bells rang and whistles filled the air. Blowing his car horn en route to Poughkeepsie, John joined the excited crowds. In his journal he wrote: "What an eventful period of the world I have lived in! I have known Emerson and Whitman. I knew Lincoln, and touched his hand. I lived through the Civil War, saw slavery crushed and disappear. And now I have lived to see *this* War end!"

During the winter of 1920, John, his granddaughter Ursula, and Clara and her two nieces, Harriet and Eleanor, traveled to California by train. Part of the time, they settled in La Jolla, staying on the estate of Ellen Browning Scripps. John's home, called Wistaria Cottage, was a short distance from the Pacific Ocean.

Visitors came to see John, and he spoke to students at several schools. He kept up his writing, especially his letter writing, sitting in a chair which overlooked the ocean. Brown pelicans and other sea birds skimmed the surf. In December he wrote a friend that La Jolla was "an earthly paradise—all sun and sky, and sea,—flowers blooming and birds singing." Trap-door spiders, which live in the sandy soil of the Southwest, fascinated him, so he spent long hours studying them in their silk-lined tunnels.

The weather turned damp and foggy along the coast. For the first time, John's health was failing. He came down with a cold and was hospitalized for a while. John grew grumpy, and instead of enjoying the seals playing in the waves and barking on the rocks, he called them the "hounds of the sea." The Pacific Ocean reminded him of a desert, "forbidding and inhospitable."

To escape the harsh winters in New York, John often traveled west. Here, he stands in front of Wistaria Cottage in La Jolla, California. The Pacific Ocean lies behind the cottage.

John longed to return home. He told Clara he missed his other grandchildren and Julian, as well as the Catskill Mountains. He ordered seeds to plant in the spring, talked about plowing the garden, and planned his eighty-fourth birthday party at Woodchuck Lodge.

With Clara, his granddaughter, and Clara's two nieces, he boarded a train in late March.

Looking thin and pale, he lay in his berth. Clara and the three girls took care of him. During the days, John stared out the window from his bed. "How far are we from home?" he asked Clara and Harriet early on the morning of March 29, as the train sped across Ohio. A few moments later, John Burroughs died.

On April 3, 1921, John was buried on the family farm next to his favorite moss-covered rock. His longtime wish had come true. "Here," he wrote in *My Boyhood,* published posthumously in 1922, "I hope to rest when my work and play are over—when the sun goes down—here by my boyhood rock." It would have been his eighty-fourth birthday. The sun beamed brightly, drying the dew-soaked grass, as the nation mourned his death and his friends and family said a final good-bye.

A friend summed up his life in a memoir, *The Seer of Slabsides*:

> John Burroughs . . . was an essayist, with a love for books only sec-
> ond to his love for nature; a watcher in the woods, a tiller of the soil,
> a reader, critic, thinker, poet, whose chief business these past sixty
> years has been the interpretation of the out-of-doors.

In an essay titled "My Father," which appeared in the second half of *My Boyhood*, Julian said: "I have always suspected that Father liked to think of himself as a bee, out in the sunshine and warmth, in the fields and woods, among the flowers, gathering delightful impressions of it all."

CHAPTER TEN

John Burroughs's Legacy

"Nature . . . is only real when you reach out and touch it with your hands," John Burroughs told a group of school children in 1912. This simple message—inviting us to step out-of-doors and experience the world of nature—makes the words and deeds of this naturalist-writer seem timeless. Friends and family agreed and in 1921, they helped to establish the John Burroughs Memorial Association (now called the John Burroughs Association) to carry this message to future generations.

On the third of April of each year—John Burroughs's birthday—the Association meets at the American Museum of Natural History in New York City to award the John Burroughs Medal, nature writing's most distinguished honor. William Beebe received the first award in 1926. Some of the subsequent winners were Rachel Carson, Paul Brooks, Ann Zwinger, Joseph Wood Krutch, Peter Mathiesson, and Roger Tory Peterson. The Association also selects several outstanding nature books for children each year.

Slabsides, John's rustic cabin, located in West Park, a mile and a half from Riverby on the Hudson River and eighty miles north of New York City, is a National Historic Landmark. The John Burroughs Association maintains the cabin and holds an open house there twice a year, on the third Saturday in May and the first Saturday in October. The John Burroughs Sanctuary, one hundred seventy acres of woodlands surrounding Slabsides, is open throughout the year.

Woodchuck Lodge, John's summer home in the Catskill Mountains, is outside the village of Roxbury in New York. The house, also a Historic Landmark, is owned by his descendants and used as a summer home. Memorial Field is one-quarter mile beyond the lodge. A footpath heads uphill to a pasture and a large boulder, the Boyhood Rock. Nearby, a knee-high stone rectangular wall marks the spot where John Burroughs is buried. The Old Home farm is past Memorial Field on the same side of the road. It is privately owned. Old Clump is also called Burroughs Mountain.

A bronze plaque is mounted on a ledge beneath a spot where John Burroughs often camped on Slide Mountain, the highest peak in New York's Catskill Mountains. The plaque says: "Here the works of man dwindle in the heart of the southern Catskills."

Acknowledgments

The author wishes to thank many people and organizations. Elizabeth Burroughs Kelley, John's first grandchild and the author of numerous books about her grandfather, graciously met me at her home at Riverby in West Park, New York. She has faithfully answered my questions and, assisted by Bill Urbin, has given me family photographs. Joan Burroughs, granddaughter of Julian Burroughs, was extremely gracious to me and my family during the Slabsides Centennial in

October of 1995. Thanks also go to Paul Brooks, editor, author, and winner of the Burroughs Medal in 1965 for *Roadless Area,* for lending me books on John Burroughs; Edward Kanze, author of *The World of John Burroughs*; Lisa Breslof, Secretary of the John Burroughs Association, Inc., in New York; staff at the American Museum of Natural History Department of Library Services, New York, for helping me view over 1,000 Burroughs-related photographs; Nancy MacKechnie, Elaine Pike, and staff at the Vassar College Library Special Collections in Poughkeepsie, New York, for letting me look at photographs and Burroughs's notebook and journals that he kept between 1876 and 1921; staff at the Catskill Center in Arkville, New York, who directed me to Woodchuck Lodge and the Boyhood Rock; Barbara Cole, owner of Cole's Book Shop in La Jolla, California, originally Wistaria Cottage; Dorothy DuMond, historian, of the Klyne Esopus Historical Society Museum in Ulster Park, New York; Dorothy Morey, niece of Francis Lee Jaques, artist and author, who won the Burroughs Medal in 1946 with his wife; Dan Lombardo, curator, and the staff at the Jones Library Special Collections in Amherst, Massachusetts; Jody Primoff in Roxbury, New York, on behalf of her mother Harriet Barrus Shatraw; Wallace Dailey, curator of the Theodore Roosevelt Collection at Harvard College in Cambridge, Massachusetts; Daryl Morrison and staff at the Holt-Atherton Special Collections, University of the Pacific Libraries in Stockton, California; my son Dan Wadsworth, for photograph research at the Library of Congress; and Bill Wadsworth, for research and photograph assistance.

Finally, I would like to thank my grandfather, Clinton Gilbert Abbott, for writing in his diary about spending a "most enjoyable day" at Slabsides on September 14, 1902, where he and his friends talked with John Burroughs about Walt Whitman and birds while preparing "chops, onions, potatoes and other delicacies, which we all helped to cook over the fire." My grandfather, then twenty-two, went on to pursue a career as a naturalist. I eventually inherited several of his favorite nature-related books, including *Under the Maples* by John Burroughs.

To learn more about the John Burroughs Association, contact:

The John Burroughs Association, Inc.
15 West 77th Street
New York, NY 10024–5192

Books by John Burroughs

All were published by Houghton Mifflin Company unless otherwise stated.

Notes on Walt Whitman As Poet and Person. New York: American News Co., 1867.

Wake-Robin. Boston: Hurd & Houghton (later Houghton Mifflin Co.), 1871.

Winter Sunshine, 1875

Birds and Poets, 1877

Locusts and Wild Honey, 1879

Pepacton, 1881

Fresh Fields, 1884

Signs and Seasons, 1886

Indoor Studies, 1889

Riverby, 1894

Whitman, A Study, 1896

The Light of Day, 1900

Literary Values, 1902

The Life of Audubon, 1902

Far and Near, 1904

Ways of Nature, 1905

Bird and Bough, 1906

Camping and Tramping with Roosevelt, 1907

Leaf and Tendril, 1908

Time and Change, 1912

The Summit of the Years, 1913

The Breath of Life, 1915

Under the Apple Trees, 1916

Field and Study, 1919

Accepting the Universe, 1920

The following books were published posthumously:

Under the Maples, 1921

The Last Harvest, 1922

My Dog Friends, 1928

With Julian Burroughs. *My Boyhood.* New York: Doubleday, Page, & Co., 1922.

Selected Bibliography

Unless otherwise stated, excerpts from John Burroughs's journals and correspondence are from *The Life and Letters of John Burroughs*, Volumes 1 and 2, by Clara Barrus.

Books for Adults

Barrus, Clara, M. D. *John Burroughs, Boy and Man.* New York: Doubleday, Page & Co., 1920.

———. *The Life and Letters of John Burroughs.* Volumes 1 and 2. Boston: Houghton Mifflin Co., 1925.

———. *Our Friend John Burroughs.* Boston: Houghton Mifflin Co., 1914.

———. *Whitman and Burroughs, Comrades.* Boston: Houghton Mifflin Co., 1931.

Brooks, Paul. *"The Two Johns: Burroughs and Muir."* In *Speaking for Nature.* San Francisco: Sierra Club Books, 1980.

Haring, H. A., ed. *The Slabsides Book of John Burroughs.* Boston: Houghton Mifflin Co., 1931.

Kanze, Edward. *The World of John Burroughs.* New York: Harry N. Abrams, 1993.

Kelley, Elizabeth Burroughs. *John Burroughs: Naturalist.* New York: Riverby Books, 1987.

Kimmel, Stanley. *Mr. Lincoln's Washington.* New York: Coward-McCann, 1957.

Kligerman, Jack, ed. *The Birds of John Burroughs.* New York: Hawthorn Books, 1976.

Marks, Alfred H., ed. *The John Burroughs Review.* New York: The John Burroughs Association, 1987.

Renehan, Edward J., Jr. *John Burroughs, An American Naturalist.* Vermont: Chelsea Green Publishing Co., 1992.

Sharp, Dallas Lore. *The Seer of Slabsides.* Boston: Houghton Mifflin Co., 1921.

Streshinsky, Shirley. *Audubon: Life and Art in the Wilderness.* New York: Villard Books, 1993.

Turner, Frederick W. *Rediscovering America: John Muir in His Times and Ours.* San Francisco: Sierra Club Books, 1985.

Whitman, Walt. *Leaves of Grass.* New York: Peter Pauper Press, 1963.

Wiley, Farida A., ed. *John Burroughs' America.* New York: Devin-Adair, 1951.

Wolfe, Linnie Marsh. *Son of the Wilderness: The Life of John Muir*. Madison: University of Wisconsin Press. 1978.

Books for Young Readers

Faber, Doris and Harold. "John Burroughs." In *Great Lives: Nature and the Environment*. New York: Charles Scribner's Sons, 1991.

Freedman, Russell. *Lincoln: A Photobiography*. New York: Clarion Books, 1987.

Reef, Catherine. *Walt Whitman*. New York: Clarion Books, 1995.

Swift, Hildegarde Hoyt. *The Edge of April: A Biography of John Burroughs*. New York: William Morrow & Co., 1957.

Wadsworth, Ginger. *John Muir: Wilderness Protector*. Minneapolis: Lerner Publications, 1992.

Photo Credits

Index